WE STRIVE FOR PEACE AND SECURITY, HEARTENED BY THE CHANGES ALL AROUND US. SINCE THE TURN OF THE CENTURY, THE NUMBER OF DEMOCRACIES IN THE WORLD HAS GROWN FOURFOLD. HUMAN FREEDOM IS ON THE MARCH, AND NOWHERE MORE SO THAN OUR OWN HEMISPHERE. FREEDOM IS ONE OF THE DEEPEST AND NOBLEST ASPIRATIONS OF THE HUMAN SPIRIT. PEOPLE, WORLDWIDE, HUNGER FOR THE RIGHT OF SELF-DETERMINATION, FOR THOSE INALIENABLE RIGHTS THAT MAKE FOR HUMAN DIGNITY AND PROGRESS.

The Deepest and Noblest Aspirations

There are no great limits to growth because there are no limits of human intelligence, imagination, and wonder.

Ronald Reagan

The Deepest and Noblest Aspirations

THE WISDOM OF RONALD REAGAN

BY THE EDITORS OF CIDER MILL PRESS

CIDER MILL PRESS

BOOK PUBLISHERS

Kennebunkport, Maine

13-Digit ISBN: 978-1-60433-137-0
10-Digit ISBN: 1-60433-137-2

This book may be ordered by mail from the publisher. Please include $3.50 for postage and handling. Please support your local bookseller first!

Books published by Cider Mill Press Book Publishers are available at special discounts for bulk purchases in the United States by corporations, institutions, and other organizations. For more information, please contact the publisher.

Cider Mill Press Book Publishers
"Where good books are ready for press"
12 Port Farm Road
Kennebunkport, Maine 04046
Visit us on the Web!
www.cidermillpress.com

Design by Ponderosa Pine Design, Vicky Vaughn Shea

Typography: Agenda, Alons Antique, Baskerville, Bickham Script, Excelsior, Freehand 521, Iowan, Myriad, Olduvai, P22 Declaration

Front cover photo by William Coupon
All photos Courtesy of Ronald Reagan Library, except for the following: pages 49, 66, 70, 153 Library of Congress, Prints and Photographs Division (19180u, 08490u, 00736u, 3c34150u); page 90 ©www.Shutterstock.com/Margoe Edwards; page 113 ©Courtesy of Coleen Thompson; page 159 POOL/AFP/Getty Images; page 160 Mark Wilson/Getty Images

Printed in Korea
1 2 3 4 5 6 7 8 9 0

First Edition

Table of Contents

Ronald Reagan wearing cowboy hat at Rancho Del Cielo, 1976.

Introduction

Aᴄᴛᴇʀ ᴀ ꜰᴜʟʟ ᴄᴀʀᴇᴇʀ ɪɴ ʙʀᴏᴀᴅᴄᴀsᴛɪɴɢ ᴀɴᴅ acting, Ronald Reagan gave the rest of his life to public service. He was the 33rd governor of California, twice elected, and served from January 3, 1967 to January 7, 1975. He then became the 40th President of the United States, serving from January 20, 1981, to January 20, 1989, also being twice elected.

From around 1964, the year Barry Goldwater's candidacy coalesced a conservative movement within the Republican ranks that altered the discourse within the Republican party, and for the next 40 years, Ronald Reagan found a voice and a cause that stayed with him the rest of his life. He dedicated himself to those conservative ideas, and he eventually proved to be the popular leader of the conservative movement as it matured in America.

Reagan was a voice for change in a time when liberal ideas had, in their own way, formed from the time of FDR's New Deal and blossomed into the New Frontier and the

Great Society. However, the biggest concerns for Reagan were a ballooning government, which had quadrupled in size in his generation's lifetime, and was in and of itself an anathema to a generation that had to pull itself up by its own bootstraps, scrimping and saving through the Great Depression, only to be rewarded with the unenviable and inevitable ordeals of World War II.

Like many of his generation and ilk, Reagan understood the value of unemployment insurance—or assistance, as it became known. During the long, painful years of the Depression, he championed such programs, which were meant to help sustain people temporarily, until they could right their own situations. But as each of these small programs grew, Reagan and other conservatives saw the blossoming of a cradle-to-grave socialist state emerge, and he watched anxiously as the federal government mushroomed seemingly overnight, becoming the leviathan that he felt the country's founding fathers were so passionately against.

> **Reagan found a voice and a cause that stayed with him the rest of his life …**

Suddenly, the capitalist system that Washington, Hamilton, Adams, and many conservative heroes had spent their lives and fortunes trying to establish was now a country run for and by the government instead of for and by the people. Reagan's clarion call—to unchain business from too many restrictions, reduce the size of the government, and return America to a powerful and strong sovereign state—was heard and embraced by millions of Americans.

While in office, Reagan and his administration put a stop to many liberal initiatives, and he launched numerous conservative programs. During his time in office, the military was improved and strengthened, communism was defeated in Iron Curtain countries and Afghanistan, the Berlin Wall

President Reagan giving a speech at the Berlin Wall, Brandenburg Gate, Federal Republic of Germany, June 12, 1987.

was on the verge of being torn down, and the Soviet Union began to unravel and dissolve. And in America? Prosperity and vast wealth returned after the days of the fuel crises, massive inflation, and huge unemployment. Pride, the American Dream, and the idea of unfettered personal ownership and freedom had been renewed. Reagan kept the faith, and America found its way back to prosperity.

Perhaps more importantly, after his time at the center of the political stage, after sixteen years as a well-known governor and president, Reagan remained a staunch and revered conservative voice and figure. And today, his words and ideals are as popular as ever.

In his lifetime, Ronald Reagan lived and extolled the American Dream. He believed that people should be free to do as they choose, unfettered by government interference. He believed that America's promise of riches for anyone who was willing to work hard enough was still the dream of millions, both in this country and around the world. He believed in a lean government. He believed in helping people but not coddling them. He believed that a strong state was a peaceful state. And he believed that conservative values were the nearest and dearest to what the America's founding fathers had envisioned.

Ronald Reagan (with "Dutch" haircut), Neil Reagan, and parents Jack and Nelle Reagan. Family Christmas card circa 1916-17.

1

On Sports

Ronald Reagan was born in Tampico, Illinois, on February 6, 1911, in an apartment above the local bank building. He was the second son of an Irish Catholic father, John Edward "Jack" Reagan, and Nelle Wilson Reagan, who was of Scottish-English descent. The Reagan's eldest son, Neil "Moon" Reagan, had been born three years earlier.

The Reagans were somewhat nomadic, moving from town to town throughout Illinois, living in such places as Monmouth, Galesburg, and Chicago. In 1919, they returned to Tampico and lived above the H.C. Pitney Variety Store. Years later, after he won the presidency and was residing in the private residential quarters upstairs in the White House, Reagan quipped to friends and visitors, that he was "living above the store again."

Jack and Nelle Reagan were outgoing people who had an active social life. They both also liked to participate in local theater. Nelle, through the church she attended, performed visitations to the sick and needy.

A plump child, Ronald looked like a "fat little Dutchman" to father Jack, who subsequently nicknamed him "Dutch." This look was enhanced by Ronald's childhood haircut, which was known as a Dutchman. The nickname stuck throughout his young life, and it followed him into manhood.

According to Paul Kengor, author of *God and Ronald Reagan*, young Ronald was baptized in 1922 in his mother's religion, the Disciples of Christ Faith. From her, he inherited a

Ronald Reagan (front row, fourth from right) and his brother, Neil Reagan, (front row, third from right) on their Dixon high school football team, Dixon, Illinois, 1925.

unflagging faith in the goodness of people. Even at an early age, Reagan felt strong opposition to racial discrimination. In one early experience in Dixon, Illinois, Reagan witnessed a local innkeeper turn away several black people. Reagan, put out by the innkeeper's actions, invited the group back to his own home. Nelle invited them to spend the night, and she fed them breakfast the next morning.

During their time in Dixon, Reagan attended Dixon High School. He developed interests in acting and sports. In 1926 at Rock River in Lowell Park outside Dixon, Reagan took a job as a lifeguard, and he saved seventy-seven swimmers. He made a notch in a log for every life he saved. Upon graduation from high school, Reagan attended Eureka College. He majored in economics and sociology, and he was very active in sports, including football. He was a member of the Tau Kappa Epsilon fraternity.

In 1932, Reagan decided to try his hand at radio broadcasting as an announcer. After graduation from Eureka College, he drove to Iowa, where he auditioned for jobs at many local radio stations. He was finally hired by the University of Iowa to announce home football games for the Hawkeyes. He was paid ten dollars per game. Not long after that, he also took on a staff announcer's position at radio station

Ronald Reagan as a WHO Radio announcer in Des Moines, Iowa, 1934-37.

WOC in Davenport, Iowa. By then, Reagan was earning $100 per month. He was so successful that he moved on to WHO radio in Des Moines, where he announced Cubs games. Reagan would receive the results of the game by wire, and he would then re-create the ball game on the air for his local listeners.

"There were several other stations broadcasting that game, and I knew I'd lose my audience if I told them we'd lost our telegraph connections, so I took a chance. I had [Billy] Jurges hit another foul. Then I had him foul one that only missed being a home run by a foot," Reagan later admitted. "I had him foul one back in the stands and took up some time describing the two lads that got in a fight over the ball. I kept on having him foul balls until I was setting a record for a ballplayer hitting successive foul balls, and I was getting more than a little scared. Just then, my operator started typing. When he passed me the paper I started to giggle. It said: 'Jurges popped out on the first ball pitched.'"

In 1937, while traveling with the Cubs in California, Reagan took a screen test. His audition went well, and Reagan landed a seven-year contract with Warner Brothers studios. Reagan made a career in what were then known as "B" movies. Years later, Reagan joked, the producers "didn't want them good, they wanted them Thursday."

By the end of 1939, Reagan had appeared in nineteen films. His first movie was a starring role in the forgettable 1937 romance *Love Is On The Air*. His first big star turn came in *Knute Rockne, All American*, where he played the role of George "The Gipper" Gipp, the late star running back of the Notre Dame

> Ronald looked like a "fat little Dutchman" to father Jack.

University football team. From that role, which was a popular one, he received a new nickname that stuck, especially through his political career: the Gipper.

In 1940, he starred in *The Santa Fe Trail*, and in 1942, he appeared in one of his biggest hits, *Kings Row*. It was undoubtedly one of his biggest movie successes, and in Reagan's own words, "made me a star."

However, his career was interrupted due to his service in World War II, when he enlisted in the U.S. Army two months after *King's Row*'s release. He never regained leading-man status, but he did appear in several films after the war, including *Tennessee's Partner, This Is the Army, Dark Victory, Bedtime for Bonzo, Cattle Queen of Montana, Hellcats of the Navy,* and *The Killers*.

Ronald Reagan flying a P-40 airplane in a still from the Army Air Force training film *Identification of a Japanese Zero*, 1943.

Going to college offered me the chance
to play football for four more years.

—from *An American Life*, by Ronald Reagan

〰

*I just know its an ugly rumor that
you [Gaylord Perry] and I are the
only two people left alive who saw Abner
Doubleday throw out the first pitch.*

—remark made to the Hall of Fame pitcher Gaylord Perry

I never cared for baseball … because I was ball-shy at batting. When I stood at the plate, the ball appeared out of nowhere about two feet in front of me. I was always the last chosen for a side in any game.

—from *An American Life*, by Ronald Reagan

I really do love baseball, and I wish we could do this out on the lawn every day.

—remarks at a ceremony observing National Amateur Baseball Month, May 11, 1983

I wouldn't even complain if a stray ball came through the Oval Office window now and then.

—remarks at a ceremony observing National Amateur Baseball Month, May 11, 1983

***Nostalgia bubbles within me, and
I might have to be dragged away.***

—statement made at a 1981 Hall of Famers'
Luncheon at the White House

∽

*One day at Catalina, Charlie Grimm,
the Cubs' manager, bawled me out for
not even showing up at the practice
field. How could I tell him that
somewhere within myself was the
knowledge I would no longer be a
sports announcer?*

—from *An American Life*, by Ronald Reagan

TOP: Ronald Reagan with his older brother Neil (Moon) Reagan. circa 1912.

LEFT: Ronald Reagan sitting (hand on chin in front row) posing with other family members, Neil Reagan at far right (front row), Jack Reagan (middle row at left), Nelle Reagan (last row, second from left), in Illinois in the 1920s.

BELOW: Ronald Reagan sitting (hand on chin in front row) with other golf caddies for the Lincoln Highway Ladies Golf Tournament, Dekalb, Illinois, 1922.

RIGHT: Ronald Reagan with mother Nelle Reagan and father Jack Reagan in California, circa 1937–38.

MIDDLE: Formal photograph of Ronald Reagan, 1934.

BOTTOM LEFT: Ronald Reagan (back row, third from left) on the Army Air Force basketball team in Culver City, California, 1943.

BOTTOM RIGHT: A Ronald Reagan still from the film *Knute Rockne-All American*, 1940.

On Freedom

ON APRIL 29, 1937, RONALD REAGAN enlisted in the U.S. Army Enlisted Reserve after completing fourteen home-study courses, and he was assigned to Troop B, 322nd Cavalry at Des Moines, Iowa. On May 25, 1937, he was appointed second lieutenant in the Officers Reserve Corps of the Cavalry, and by June 18, he was assigned to the 323rd Cavalry.

On April 18, 1942, Reagan was ordered to active duty in the U.S. Army. Reagan was nearsighted, and so he was classified for limited service only. He was excluded from serving overseas. He reported for his first assignment at the San Francisco Port of Embarkation at Fort Mason, California. He was a liaison officer of the Port and Transportation Office.

On May 15, 1942, Reagan applied for and was accepted

Lieutenant Ronald Reagan posing with his mother Nelle, circa 1940s.

to transfer to the Army Air Force, where he was assigned to AAF Public Relations and subsequently to the 1st Motion Picture Unit (officially, the 18th AAF Base Unit) in Culver City, California. He was promoted to captain on July 22, 1943. His unit made training films for the army.

In January 1944, in New York City, Captain Reagan's star power was harnessed in the war effort, when he was asked to participate in the sixth War Loan Drive opening ceremonies. He returned to Fort MacArthur, California, where he was separated from active duty on December 9, 1945. Reagan's units had produced some 400 training films for the AAF by war's end.

"Ronald Reagan spoke about ground-breaking ideas, and Reagan's speeches almost always focused on individual freedom and hope," says *Conservatism Today*.

> Freedom is one of the deepest and noblest aspirations of the human spirit.
>
> —from the second inaugural address, January 21, 1985

Freedom prospers when religion
is vibrant and the rule of law under
God is acknowledged.

—remark at the annual convention of the National
Association of Evangelicals, March 8, 1983

The poet called Miss Liberty's torch "the lamp beside the golden door." Well, that was the entrance to America, and it still is. And now you really know why we're here tonight. The glistening hope of that lamp is still ours. Every promise, every opportunity, is still golden in this land. And through that golden door our children can walk into tomorrow with the knowledge that no one can be denied the promise that is America. Her heart is full; her torch is still golden, her future bright. She has arms big enough to comfort and strong enough to support, for the strength in her arms is the strength of her people. She will carry on in the '80s unafraid, unashamed, and unsurpassed. In this springtime of hope, some lights seem eternal; America's is.

—in a speech to the Republican National Convention, August 23, 1984

Captain Ronald Reagan in the Army Air Force, working for the 1st Motion Picture Unit in Culver City, California, 1943–44.

We have found in our country that, when people have the right to make decisions as close to home as possible, they usually make the right decisions.

—Address to the International Committee for the Supreme Soviet of the U.S.S.R., September 17, 1990

Information is the oxygen of the modern age. It seeps through the walls topped by barbed wire, it wafts across the electrified borders. The Goliath of totalitarianism will be brought down by the David of the microchip.

—as quoted in *The Guardian*, June 14, 1989

༄

Freedom is the right to question and change the established way of doing things. It is the continuous revolution of the marketplace. It is the understanding that allows us to recognize shortcomings and seek solutions.

—address at Moscow State University, May 31, 1988

I've spoken of the shining city all my political life. And how stands the city on this winter night? After 200 years, two centuries, she still stands strong and true to the granite ridge, and her glow has held, no matter what storm. And she's still a beacon, still a magnet for all who must have freedom, for all the pilgrims from all the lost places who are hurtling through the darkness, toward home.

—farewell address to the nation, January 11, 1989

One legislator accused me of having a nineteenth-century attitude on law and order. That is a totally false charge. I have an eighteenth-century attitude. Freedom is never more than one generation away from extinction. We didn't pass it on to our children in the bloodstream. It must be fought for, protected, and handed on for them to do the same, or one day we will spend our sunset years telling our children what it was once like in the United States when men were free.

—Address to the Phoenix Chamber of Commerce, March 30, 1961

I'm convinced that today the majority of Americans want what those first Americans wanted: a better life for themselves and their children; a minimum of government authority. There are those in America today who have come to depend absolutely on government for their security. And when government fails, they seek to rectify that failure in the form of granting government more power. So, as government has failed to control crime and violence with the means given it by the Constitution, they seek to give it more power at the expense of the Constitution. But in doing so, in their willingness to give up their arms in the name of safety, they are really giving up their protection from what has always been the chief source of despotism: government. Lord Acton said power corrupts. Surely, then, if this is true, the more power we give the government, the more corrupt it will become. And if we give it the power to confiscate our arms, we also give up the ultimate means to combat that corrupt power. In doing so, we can only assure that we will eventually be totally subject to it. When dictators come to power, the first thing they do is take away the people's weapons. It makes it so much easier for the secret police to operate, it makes it so much easier to force the will of the ruler upon the ruled.

—from a column published in *Guns and Ammo*, September 1975

Abraham Lincoln freed the black man. In many ways, Dr. King freed the white man. How did he accomplish this tremendous feat? Where others—white and black—preached hatred, he taught the principles of love and nonviolence. We can be so thankful that Dr. King raised his mighty eloquence for love and hope rather than for hostility and bitterness. He took the tension he found in our nation, a tension of injustice, and channeled it for the good of America and all her people.

—Address on the anniversary of the birth of
Martin Luther King, Jr., January 15, 1983

President Reagan signs the Reparations Bill for Japanese-Americans in the Old Executive Office Building, August 10, 1988.

Blood that has soaked into the sands of a beach is all of one color. America stands unique in the world: the only country not founded on race but on a way, an ideal. Not in spite of, but because of, our polyglot background, we have had all the strength in the world. That is the American way.

—statement made while signing the bill providing restitution for the wartime internment of Japanese-American civilians, August 10, 1988

Ronald Reagan testifying at the House Un-American Activities Committee (HUAC) hearings in Washington, DC. October 25, 1947.

On Communism

IN 1941, RONALD REAGAN WAS ELECTED TO serve as an alternate on the board of directors of the Screen Actors Guild (SAG). After serving in the war effort, he resumed service on the SAG board, and became 3rd vice president in 1946. In 1947, the SAG president and six board members were forced to resign due to the adoption of conflict-of-interest bylaws. Reagan was nominated in a special election for the position of president and was subsequently elected. He served seven additional one-year terms, from 1947 to 1952 and was elected once again in 1959. Reagan led SAG through eventful years that were marked by labor-management disputes, the Taft-Hartley Act, the House Committee on Un-American Activities

(HUAC) hearings, and the Hollywood blacklist era.

While still a Democrat politically, Reagan was always a fervent anticommunist. He publicly reaffirmed his commitment to democratic principles, saying, "I never as a citizen want to see our country become urged, by either fear or resentment of this group, that we ever compromise with any of our democratic principles through that fear or resentment."

During the Red Scare, Reagan did all he believed he could do to be a good American, working with the FBI and

Ronald Reagan and *General Electric Theater*. 1954–62.

testifying openly before the House Un-American Activities Committee on the subject as well. This sometimes made him a subject of scourge with his more liberal friends in film and television, but Reagan always stood by his actions, claiming his intentions were good and honorable and in the best interests of the country.

In the 1950s, Reagan joined the increasingly popular television medium. In the 1950s, he was the host of *General Electric Theater*, which paid him a princely fee of $125,000 per year. As part of his contract with the series, he was obligated to tour GE plants ten weeks out of the year. This sometimes obliged him to make up to four-teen speeches per day. His final work as a professional actor was

Reagan was always a fervent anti-communist.

as host and performer from 1964 to 1965 on the television series *Death Valley Days*.

"I learned something new about Reagan's lifetime cru-sade against communism," said historian and writer Paul Kengor, author of *The Crusader: Ronald Reagan and the Fall of Communism*, "about his eloquent leadership against the attempted communist takeover of Hollywood's trade unions after World War II; about his insightful analysis of the aims and weaknesses of the Soviet Union before he entered the White House; about his understanding that Poland could be the wedge that knocked apart the evil empire, and of his close relationship with Pope John Paul II—I had no idea until I read Paul's book that the president and the pope had met at least seven times."

"In the 1980s, we placed our hopes in Ronald Reagan and Margaret Thatcher. The fact that someone out there called communism by its proper name and actually did something to promote freedom and democracy helped us a great deal," said Senator Jan Ruml, a former Czechoslovak anticommunist dissident who was serving a prison sentence during the 1980s. "Ronald Reagan was the man instrumental in bringing down communism, and we should all remember him with great respect as the man, thanks to whom we are enjoying our present freedom."

"Ronald Reagan," said Jiri Dienstbier, former Czechoslovak foreign minister, "was a very controversial person even in America. He had very strong conservative rightist rhetoric, but in fact he behaved very pragmatically. He spoke about the evil empire, but then he walked with Mikhail Gorbachev in the Red Square because he understood that a lot of things had changed in Russia, and America should support it."

"The dialogue that President Reagan and I started was difficult. To reach agreement, particularly on arms control and security, we had to overcome mistrust and the barriers

> Here's my strategy on the Cold War: We win, they lose.
> —first cabinet meeting as President, January 1981

President Reagan and Soviet General Secretary Gorbachev meet in the boathouse during the Geneva Summit in Switzerland, November 15, 1985

of numerous problems and prejudices," wrote former Soviet Prime Minister Mikhail Gorbachev in *A President Who Listened*. "I don't know whether we would have been able to agree and to insist on the implementation of our agreements with a different person at the helm of American government. True, Reagan was a man of the right. But, while adhering to his convictions, with which one could agree or disagree, he was not dogmatic; he was looking for negotiations and cooperation. And this was the most important thing to me: he had the trust of the American people."

"Reagan bolstered the U.S. military might to ruin the Soviet economy, and he achieved his goal," said former Soviet foreign ministry spokesman Gennady Gerasimov.

But *The Economist* said it best, summing up Reagan's efforts combating communism, writing in 2004, "By defeating communism, Ronald Reagan ended one of history's most violent centuries and opened the door to the possibility that, for at least a few decades ahead, war, though it can never be abolished, would be a smaller horror than in the past, and democracy might become available to more of the people who wanted it. In his foreign policy, at any rate, he turned out to be one of the two or three most effective American presidents of the twentieth century."

> *It is the Soviet Union that runs against the tide of history . . . [It is] the march of freedom and democracy which will leave Marxism-Leninism on the ash heap of history as it has left other tyrannies which stifle the freedom and muzzle the self-expression of the people.*
> —from a speech to Britain's Parliament, 1982

President Reagan giving a speech at the Commencement ceremony at University of Notre Dame in South Bend, Indiana, May 17, 1981.

The years ahead will be great ones for our country, for the cause of freedom and the spread of civilization. The West will not contain communism; it will transcend communism. We will not bother to denounce it. We'll dismiss it as a sad, bizarre chapter in human history whose last pages are even now being written.

—from a speech at Notre Dame University, May 17, 1981

Let us beware that while [Soviet rulers] preach the supremacy of the state, declare its omnipotence over individual man, and predict its eventual domination over all the peoples of the earth, they are the focus of evil in the modern world... I urge you to beware the temptation... to ignore the facts of history and the aggressive impulses of any evil empire, to simply call the arms race a giant misunderstanding and thereby remove yourself from the struggle between right and wrong, good and evil.

—from a speech to the National Association of Evangelicals,
March 8, 1983

How do you tell a communist? Well, it's someone who reads Marx and Lenin. And how do you tell an anticommunist? It's someone who understands Marx and Lenin.

—remark in Arlington, Virginia, September 25, 1987

If the Soviet Union let another political party come into existence, they would still be a one-party state, because everybody would join the other party.

—remark to Polish Americans in Chicago, June 23, 1983

Trust, but verify.

—as quoted in the *New York Times*, December 4, 1987

President Reagan giving a speech at the Berlin Wall, Brandenburg Gate, Federal Republic of Germany, June 12, 1987.

Mr. Gorbachev, open this gate! Mr. Gorbachev, tear down this wall!

—from a speech near the Berlin Wall, June 1987

4

On Politics

THROUGHOUT HIS EARLY YEARS, REAGAN was a registered Democrat. He was a supporter of the New Deal and an admirer of President Franklin D. Roosevelt. While remaining a Democrat in the early 1950s, Reagan's political leanings began to shift. These leanings confirmed themselves in his endorsement of the presidential candidacies of Dwight D. Eisenhower in 1952 and 1956, and Richard Nixon's failed run in 1960, even though Reagan remained a Democrat.

In his position with General Electric, Reagan was required to tour GE plants around the country and deliver speeches to the employees. Often, these speeches were politically motivated and held a conservative, pro-business message. Laboring daily and diligently, Reagan wrote his own speeches. He worked hard on them, putting as much thought

Governor Ronald Reagan and Nancy Reagan at the Governor's Inaugural Ball in Sacramento, California, January 1971

into them as possible. Despite having speech writers later in the White House, he continued editing, and even occasionally writing, many of his speeches throughout his life.

By the late 1950s and early 1960s, Reagan's ideals became too controversial for GE's liking. The company thought the actor's speeches were too political, so Reagan was fired by General Electric in 1962.

Reagan formally switched to the Republican party the same year he and GE parted company. Reagan clearly and unapologetically stated, "I didn't leave the Democratic Party. The party left me." He then launched himself into the world of politics. It would become his second career, and in effect, it would be his most successful. Reagan put everything he had learned in his first career—poise, speaking, entertaining, acting, staging, and speech giving—to great use over the next thirty years. This experience would serve him well, and it would help him pave the way to great accomplishments in the world of politics.

> "Politics is not a bad profession. If you succeed, there are many rewards; if you disgrace yourself, you can always write a book."

REAGAN-BUSH '84

Bringing America Back!

A campaign poster showing head-and-shoulders portraits of Ronald Reagan and George Bush, and the facade of the White House, 1984.

Politics is just like show business. You have a hell of an opening, coast for a while, and then have a hell of a close.

—remark to Stuart Spencer 1966

How can a president not be an actor?

—response when asked how an actor could become president

[Baseball is] our national pastime, that is, if you discount political campaigning.

—remark at a ceremony observing National Amateur Baseball Month, May 11, 1983

Politics is supposed to be the second oldest profession. I have come to realize that it bears a very close resemblance to the first. I'm convinced that today the majority of Americans want what those first Americans wanted: a better life for themselves and their children; a minimum of government authority. Very simply, they want to be left alone in peace and safety to take care of the family by earning an honest dollar and putting away some savings. This may not sound too exciting, but there is something magnificent about it. On the farm, on the street corner, in the factory, and in the kitchen, millions of us ask nothing more, but certainly nothing less, than to live our own lives according to our values—at peace with ourselves, our neighbors, and the world.

—from a nationally televised address, July 6, 1976

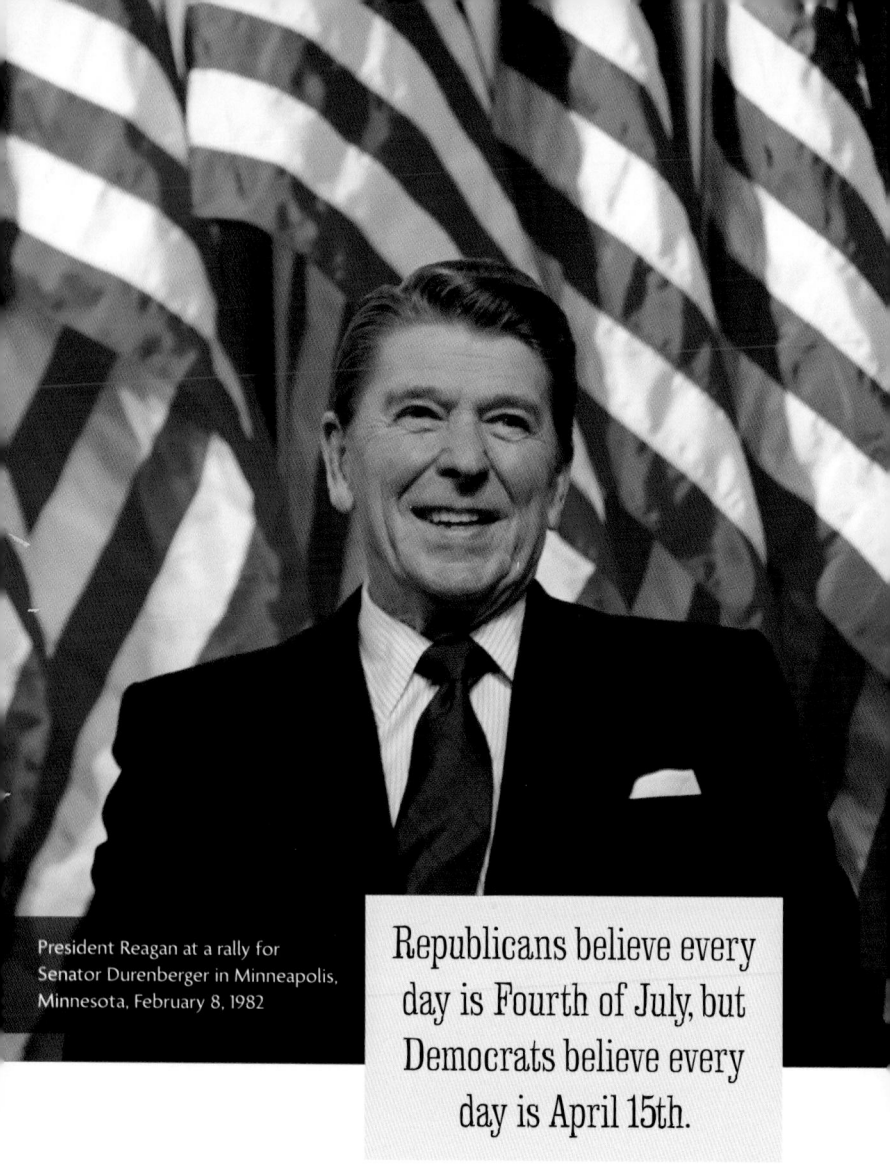

President Reagan at a rally for Senator Durenberger in Minneapolis, Minnesota, February 8, 1982

Republicans believe every day is Fourth of July, but Democrats believe every day is April 15th.

Yes, because for years
I was a Democrat.

—in response to Sam Donaldson on whether Reagan shared
any blame for the ongoing recession, September 1982

The trouble with our liberal friends is
not that they're ignorant: It's just that they
know so much that isn't so.

—from A Time for Choosing, aka "The Speech"

We're the party that wants
to see an America in which
people can still get rich.

—remarks at the Republican Congressional Salute to Ronald Reagan
dinner, May 4, 1982

President Reagan at Ashford
Castle in Ireland, June 2. 1984

This fellow they've nominated claims he's the new Thomas Jefferson. Well let me tell you something: I knew Thomas Jefferson. He was a friend of mine, and, Governor: You're no Thomas Jefferson!

—from a speech at the 1992 Republican National Convention (modeled after Lloyd Bentsen's jibe at Dan Quayle during a debate in 1988).

Let it show on the record that when the American people cried out for economic help, Jimmy Carter took refuge behind a dictionary. Well, if it's a definition he wants, I'll give him one. A recession is when your neighbor loses his job. A depression is when you lose yours. And recovery is when Jimmy Carter loses his.

—in response to Jimmy Carter's assertion that Reagan misuses the word *depression*. (1977)

[The Democrats] say that the United States
has had its days in the sun, that our nation has
passed its zenith . . . My fellow citizens,
I utterly reject that view.

—from Reagan's acceptance speech at the Republican
National Convention, July 17, 1980

The future doesn't belong to the
fainthearted, it belongs to the brave.
I intend to go right on appointing
highly qualified individuals of
the highest personal integrity
to the bench, individuals who
understand the danger of short-
circuiting the electoral process and
disenfranchising the people through
judicial activism.

—remarks during a White House briefing for United States attorneys,
October, 21, 1985

Our friends in the other party will never forgive us for our success and are doing everything in their power to rewrite history. Listening to the liberals, you'd think that the 1980s were the worst period since the Great Depression, filled with suffering and despair. I don't know about you, but I'm getting awfully tired of the whining voices from the White House these days. They're claiming there was a decade of greed and neglect, but you and I know better than that. We were there.

—remarks from the Republican National Convention annual gala, February 3, 1994

Liberals fought poverty,
and poverty won.

—as quoted in *The Right Nation: Conservative Power in America*
by John Micklethwait and Adrian Wooldridge

There you go again.

—Presidential debate, October 28, 1980, in response to criticism by
Carter about Reagan's position on Medicare

❧

Next Tuesday, all of you will go to
the polls, will stand there in the
polling place, and make a decision.
I think when you make that
decision, it might be well if you
would ask yourself, are you better
off than you were four years ago?

—remark made while campaigning for president, 1980

Ronald Reagan and Nancy Reagan aboard a boat in California. August 1964.

On Conservatism and Government

"**E**VERYONE ON THE RIGHT HAS LONG CLAIMED Ronald Reagan as his intellectual forbearer," wrote Donald Devine, editor for the American Conservative Union Foundation. "Whatever the brand of conservatism, whether it is the neoconservative love of national greatness, the paleoconservative distrust of too much freedom, the Tory-conservative suspicion of abstract philosophizing, the progressive-conservative love of big government, or the mainline-conservative fear of being thought uncompassionate—all of these claim President Reagan as their intellectual patrimony. This is not surprising since he has been the most successful conservative of modern times."

In 1964, Barry Goldwater, a U.S. senator from the state of Arizona, had fought off the venerable Nelson Rockefeller, governor of New York, in a brutal battle for the presidential candidacy. What was more at stake was the fight for the soul of the Republican Party.

Rockefeller was a liberal northeastern Republican. He was a member of the party elite. Goldwater stood for the new brand of conservatism. The conservatives, up to this time, had been a fringe group within the party, but Goldwater's huge win in a bitterly fought primary turned the tide, and in a way it changed the party's philosophy for decades to come.

"Entrepreneurs and their small enterprises are responsible for almost all the economic growth in the United States."

Reagan joined the campaign of conservative presidential contender Barry Goldwater in 1964. Speaking on Goldwater's behalf, Reagan stressed his belief in the importance of smaller government.

Reagan clearly stated his ideological motivation during the campaign in a famed speech delivered on October 27,

Ronald Reagan giving a speech for Barry Goldwater's presidential campaign at the International Hotel in Los Angeles, 1964.

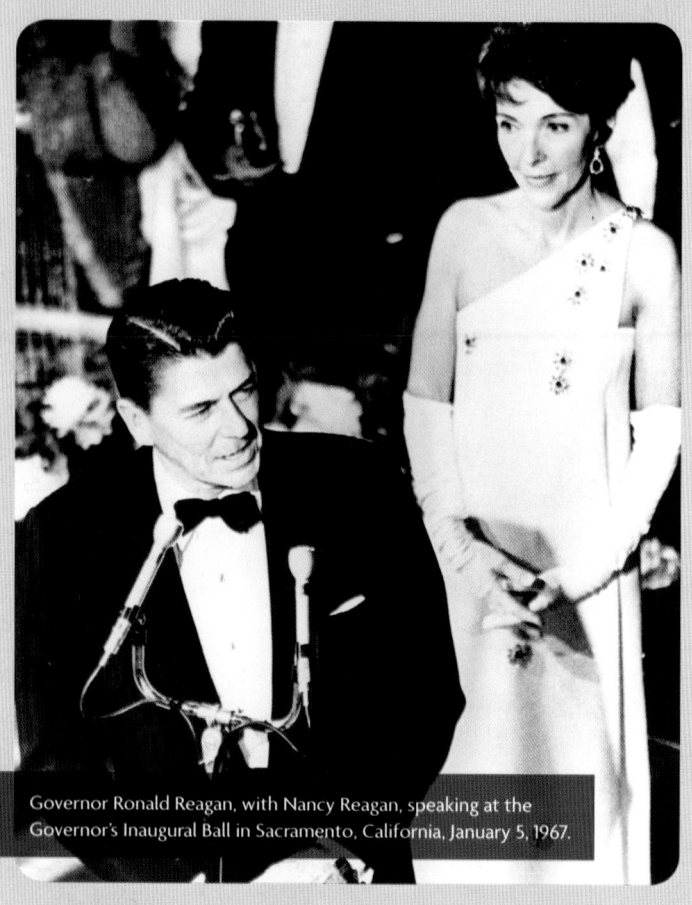

Governor Ronald Reagan, with Nancy Reagan, speaking at the Governor's Inaugural Ball in Sacramento, California, January 5, 1967.

We must reject the idea that every time a law is broken, society is guilty rather than the lawbreaker. It is time to restore the American precept that each individual is accountable for his actions.

1964: "The founding fathers knew that government can't control the economy without controlling people. And they knew when a government sets out to do that, it must use force and coercion to achieve its purpose. So we have come to a time for choosing."

Reagan made the speech, which was paid for by California businessmen, to support Goldwater's candidacy. Funds for Goldwater's campaign were at a low. Goldwater himself was not sure of Reagan's endorsement, and he tried to talk Reagan out of delivering a broadcast version of the speech. Reagan told Goldwater the speech would work, that he had given a variant of it before, and that the time was already paid for at the station. Goldwater's worries were baseless. Several hours after Reagan's speech was over, Reagan had raised almost $1,000,000 for Goldwater's cause, and he had cemented himself as a leader in the conservative movement.

> *Remember when we were a collection of little old ladies in tennis shoes and ultra-right-wing kooks? We've become respectable.*
>
> —from an address to the New York Conservative Party, January 1980

The "Time for Choosing" speech is considered to be the event that launched Ronald Reagan's political career.

President Gerald Ford and Ronald Reagan stand at the podium at the Republican National Convention, Kansas City, Missouri, August 1976.

If you analyze it, I believe the very heart and soul of conservatism is libertarianism. I think conservatism is really a misnomer just as liberalism is a misnomer for the liberals—if we were back in the days of the Revolution, so-called conservatives today would be the Liberals and the liberals would be the Tories. The basis of conservatism is a desire for less government interference or less centralized authority or more individual freedom, and this is a pretty general description also of what libertarianism is. Now, I can't say that I will agree with all the things that the present group who call themselves Libertarians in the sense of a party say, because I think that, like in any political movement, there are shades, and there are libertarians who are almost over at the point of wanting no government at all or anarchy. I believe there are legitimate government functions. There is a legitimate need in an orderly society for some government to maintain freedom, or we will have tyranny by individuals. The strongest man on the block will run the neighborhood. We have government to insure that we don't each one of us have to carry a club to defend ourselves. But again, I stand on my statement that I think that libertarianism and conservatism are traveling the same path.

—from an interview published in *Reason*, July 1975

Unemployment insurance is a pre-paid vacation for freeloaders.

—as quoted in the *Sacramento Bee*, April 28, 1966

Today, if you invent a better mousetrap, the government comes along with a better mouse.

—from a White House conference, March 14, 1985

The best minds are not in government. If any were, business would steal them away.

Government does not solve problems;
it subsidizes them.

—from *Speaking My Mind*

I'm convinced that today the majority of Americans want what those first Americans wanted: a better life for themselves and their children; a minimum of government authority.

—from a nationally televised address in 1976

President Ronald Reagan, at his desk in the Oval Office, speaking with Republican Senator John McCain of Arizona, Washington, D.C., 1987

The nearest thing to eternal life we will ever see on this earth is a government program.

—from *Speaking My Mind*

Man is not free unless government is limited.

—from *Speaking My Mind*

The taxpayer—that's someone who works for the federal government but doesn't have to take a civil-service exam.

—from a speech at the Republican National Convention,
October 27, 1964

The best social program is a productive job for anyone who's willing to work.

—remarks at a luncheon in Baltimore, July 13, 1982

Millions of individuals making their own decisions in the marketplace will always allocate resources better than any centralized government planning process.

—remarks at a World Bank Group/International Monetary Fund
meeting, September 27, 1983

If I could paraphrase a well-known statement by Will Rogers that he never met a man he didn't like—I'm afraid we have some people around here who never met a tax they didn't like.

—address to the nation on federal tax reduction legislation, July 27, 1981

We don't have a trillion-dollar debt because we haven't taxed enough; we have a trillion-dollar debt because we spend too much.

—address to the National Association of Realtors, March 28, 1982

Government exists to protect us from each other. Where government has gone beyond its limits is in deciding to protect us from ourselves.

One way to make sure crime doesn't pay would be to let the government run it.

—from 1967

Government's first duty is to protect the people, not run their lives.

—remarks at the national conference of the Building and Construction Trades, AFL-CIO, March 30, 1981

Governments tend not to solve problems,
only rearrange them.

*I have wondered at times what the Ten
Commandments would have looked like if
Moses had run them through the U.S. Congress.*

The ten most dangerous words in
the English language are
"Hi, I'm from the government,
and I'm here to help."

—remarks to Future Farmers of America, July 28, 1988

Although I held public office for a total of sixteen years, I also thought of myself as a citizen-politician, not a career one. Every now and then when I was in government, I would remind my associates that when we start thinking of government as "us" instead of "them," we've been here too long. By that, I mean that elected officeholders need to retain a certain skepticism about the perfectibility of government.

—address to the Los Angeles Junior Chamber
of Commerce, July 10, 1991

Government's view of the economy could be summed up in a few short phrases: If it moves, tax it. If it keeps moving, regulate it. And if it stops moving, subsidize it.

—remark to the White House Conference on
Small Business, August 15, 1986

And I have to point out that government doesn't tax to get the money it needs, government always needs the money it gets.

—from the Bush-Reagan debate on taxes, April 24, 1980

❧

This is not the time for political fun and games. This is the time for a new beginning. I ask you now to put aside any feelings of frustration or helplessness about our political institutions and join me in this dramatic but responsible plan to reduce the enormous burden of federal taxation on you and your family.

—address to the nation, July 27, 1981

President Reagan working alone in the Oval Office, April 24, 1981

The size of the federal budget is not an appropriate barometer of social conscience or charitable concern.

—from an address to the National Alliance of Business, October 5, 1981

It is not my intention to do away with government. It is rather to make it work—work with us, not over us; stand by our side, not ride on our back. Government can and must provide opportunity, not smother it; foster productivity, not stifle it. This administration's objective will be a healthy, vigorous, growing economy.

—from the first inaugural address, January 20, 1981

Government growing beyond our consent had become a lumbering giant, slamming shut the gates of opportunity, threatening to crush the very roots of our freedom. What brought America back? The American people brought us back—with quiet courage and common sense; with undying faith that in this nation under God, the future will be ours, for the future belongs to the free.

—from the State of the Union address February 4, 1986

Government is like a baby: an alimentary canal with a big appetite at one end and no responsibility at the other.

—joke made during the 1965 campaign for governor of California

The basis of conservatism is a desire for less government interference or less centralized authority or more individual freedom—and this is a pretty general description also of what libertarianism is.

—from an interview with the *Los Angeles Times*, January 7, 1970

One legislator accused me of having a nineteenth-century attitude on law and order. That is a totally false charge. I have an eighteenth-century attitude. That is when the founding fathers made it clear that the safety of law-abiding citizens should be one of the government's primary concerns.

—address to the Republican State Central Committee Convention, September 7, 1973

Back in 1927, an American socialist, Norman Thomas, six times candidate for president on the Socialist Party ticket, said that the American people would never vote for socialism, but he said under the name of liberalism, the American people would adopt every fragment of the socialist program.

—from the Operation Coffee Cup campaign against the social insurance program that later became known as Medicare, 1961

One of the traditional methods of imposing statism or socialism on a people has been by way of medicine. It's very easy to disguise a medical program as a humanitarian project . . . . Now, the American people, if you put it to them about socialized medicine and gave them a chance to choose, would unhesitatingly vote against it. We have an example of this. Under the Truman administration, it was proposed that we have a compulsory health insurance program for all people in the United States, and, of course, the American people unhesitatingly rejected this.

—from the Operation Coffee Cup campaign against the social insurance program that later became known as Medicare, 1961

The doctor begins to lose freedom. . . . First you decide that the doctor can have so many patients. They are equally divided among the various doctors by the government. But then doctors aren't equally divided geographically. So a doctor decides he wants to practice in one town, and the government has to say to him, "You can't live in that town. They already have enough doctors. You have to go someplace else." And from here it's only a short step to dictating where he will go. . . . All of us can see what happens once you establish the precedent that the government can determine a man's working place and his working methods, determine his employment. From here it's a short step to all the rest of socialism, to determining his pay. And pretty soon, your son won't decide, when he's in school, where he will go or what he will do for a living. He will wait for the government to tell him where he will go to work and what he will do.

—from the Operation Coffee Cup campaign against the social insurance program that later became known as Medicare, 1961

President Reagan at Rancho
Cel Cielo, April 8, 1985

I have only one thing to say to the tax
increasers: Go ahead, make my day.

—speech threatening to veto legislation raising taxes, March 13, 1985

6

On Faith and Courage

AFTER HIS "TIME FOR CHOOSING" SPEECH IN the mid-1960s, Ronald Reagan's political star rose quickly in the California political scene. He made an impression on influential California Republicans. His charisma and views were powerful, so much so that he was nominated for governor of California in 1966. Reagan's two biggest messages were that he would return those riding on the government's back via the welfare program back to work, and that he would "clean up the mess at Berkeley," referring to the student protests of the period at the University of California, Berkeley.

Ronald Reagan and Nancy Reagan at the victory celebration for California governor at the Biltmore Hotel in Los Angeles , California, November 8, 1966

He became so popular that he defeated two-term governor Edmund G. "Pat" Brown, and he was sworn in on January 3, 1967. Reagan went quickly to work, righting the wrongs he felt had laid California low. First, he froze state government hiring, immediately stopping the state government's growth. Second, he approved a series of tax hikes in order to balance the state's budget.

Reagan's reputation for fighting the increasing number of protests made him popular with many voters, who felt the protests were getting out of hand. Reagan was involved in high-profile conflicts with the protest movements of the era.

Ronald Reagan being sworn in as Governor of California by Associate Justice Marshall McComb in the State Capitol, Sacramento, California, January 2, 1967

While Reagan was governor, the national debate on abortion was just beginning. Though he felt compelled to sign an early bill regarding abortion, he quickly changed his mind, and he became an avowed anti-abortion, pro-life candidate. It was a position he would hold passionately for the remainder of his political career and for the rest of his life. He was re-elected to the governorship in 1970, defeating "Big Daddy" Jesse Unruh. He chose not to seek a third term.

Reagan's terms as governor helped to shape the policies he would pursue later in his political career as president. Reagan clarified his stance on the growth of the government and on the welfare state. He also began to clarify the Republican ideal of less government regulation of the economy, including that of undue federal taxation.

In his two terms as governor, Reagan found his political voice, the audience who heeded it, and his political conscience. It was a set of tools that would serve him well as president.

Wrote John Patrick Diggins in *Ronald Reagan: Fate, Freedom, and the Making of History:* "The genius of Ronald Reagan was, like that of Emerson, to persuade us that we please God by pleasing ourselves and that to believe in the self is to live within the divine soul."

Recognizing the equality of all men and women, we are willing and able to lift the weak, cradle those who hurt, and nurture the bonds that tie us together as one nation under God.

—address accepting the Republican presidential nomination,
August 23, 1984

We are never defeated unless we give up on God.

—remark from 1984

Let us be sure that those who come after will say of us in our time that we did everything that could be done. We finished the race; we kept them free; we kept the faith.

—from the third State of the Nation address, 1984

Within the covers of the Bible are the answers for all the problems men face.

[Evolution] has in recent years been challenged in the world of science and is not yet believed in the scientific community to be as infallible as it once was believed. But if it was going to be taught in the schools, then I think that also the biblical theory of creation, which is not a theory but the biblical story of creation, should also be taught.

—at a press conference in Dallas, Texas, August 22, 1980

Without God, democracy will not and cannot long endure.

—remarks at an ecumenical prayer breakfast, Dallas, August 23, 1984

Each generation goes further than the generation preceding it because it stands on the shoulders of that generation. You will have opportunities beyond anything we've ever known.

Freedom prospers when religion is vibrant and the rule of law under God is acknowledged.

—remarks at the National Association of Evangelicals convention, March 8, 1983

With regard to the freedom of the individual for choice with regard to abortion, there's one individual who's not being considered at all. That's the one who is being aborted. And I've noticed that everybody that is for abortion has already been born.

—from the Anderson-Reagan presidential debate, September 21, 1980

If we ever forget that we are one nation under God, then we will be a nation gone under.

—as quoted in *The Forgotten Roots of American Freedom*

❦

America's best days are yet to come. Our proudest moments are yet to be. Our most glorious achievements are just ahead. I know in my heart that man is good, that what is right will always eventually triumph. And there's purpose and worth to each and every life.

—at the dedication of the Ronald Reagan Presidential Library, November 4, 1991

❦

I wish you a lifetime of happiness and can assure you marriage is the best way to achieve that. Thomas Jefferson said, "Happiness in the married state is a blessing to be desired above all others." Now I didn't hear Jefferson say that, but I know he's right. Ignore all the cynical jokes about marriage, a man can't be complete without it. It's worth working at, and the more you work at it, the more happiness you'll have.

—Ronald Reagan to Scott Ayers, June 6, 1983

President Reagan and Mrs. Reagan pose on the White House south lawn, November 21, 1981

There is no greater happiness for a man than approaching a door at the end of a day, knowing someone on the other side of that door is waiting for the sound of his footsteps.

—from a letter to son Michael, June 13, 1971

The man who puts into the marriage only half of what he owns will get that out.

—from a letter to son Michael, June 13, 1971

Heroes may not be braver than anyone else. They're just braver five minutes longer.

Don't be afraid to see what you see.

—from the farewell address to the nation, January 11, 1989

There are no easy answers, but there are simple answers. We must have the courage to do what we know is morally right.

—from the "Time for Choosing" speech, 1964

[N]o arsenal or no weapon in the arsenals of the world is so formidable as the will and moral courage of free men and women.

—from the first inaugural address, January 20, 1981

You and I have a rendezvous with destiny. We will preserve for our children this, the last best hope of man on earth, or we will sentence them to take the first step into a thousand years of darkness. If we fail, at least let our children and our children's children say of us we justified our brief moment here. We did all that could be done.

—from "The Speech" October 27, 1964

In closing, let me thank you, the American people, for giving me the great honor of allowing me to serve as your president. When the Lord calls me home, whenever that day may be, I will leave with the greatest love for this country of ours and eternal optimism for its future. I now begin the journey that will lead me into the sunset of my life. I know that for America there will always be a bright dawn ahead.

—from his letter to the American people revealing his Alzheimer's diagnosis, November 5, 1994

Ronald Reagan giving his acceptance speech at the Republican National Convention, Detroit, Michigan, July 17, 1980

7

On Economics

In the 1976 presidential election, President Gerald Ford was the incumbent. However, with Ford struggling in the polls, Reagan made a strong bid to unseat him. He was clearly the conservative choice, with Ford being cast as the moderate Republican.

Reagan's campaign worked hard to steal early wins in North Carolina, Texas, and California, which hobbled the Ford re-election bid. But Reagan found the office of the Presidency a hard bully-pulpit to go up against, and he ended up losing New Hampshire and Florida. By convention time, Ford had surpassed Reagan and won with 1,187 delegates to Reagan's 1,070.

Reagan's concession speech was a big hit with the

Republican right. He warned about the dangers of nuclear war and about the threat posed by the Soviet Union.

Reagan again ran for the presidency in 1980. At a time when it seemed that runaway inflation could not go any higher, when unemployment was exploding, and gas prices were skyrocketing, Reagan continued to stick to those fundamental issues that were important to him: strong defense against the Soviet Union and communist influences; less government interference in people's lives; lower taxes; and a strong anti-abortion stance.

Reagan won the Republican nomination, and chose one of his primary opponents, George H.W. Bush, to be his running mate. Reagan was tremendous on television. He was affable, funny, serious, and well spoken. Whether in debate or campaigning, Reagan was a natural on television. On election day, Reagan received 50.7 percent of the popular vote while Carter took 41 percent, and Independent John B. Anderson (a liberal Republican) received 6.7 percent.

"Reagan is clearly telling many Republicans what they most want to hear, and if others are now sounding almost equally conservative, Reagan has been preaching his views longer and louder than anyone else," reported *Time* magazine on March 10, 1980.

Ronald Reagan campaigning with Nancy Reagan in Columbia, South Carolina, October 10, 1980

Inflation is as violent as a mugger, as frightening as an armed robber, and as deadly as a hit man.

—remark made in 1978

We don't have an option of living with inflation and its attendant tragedy. . . . We have an alternative, and that is the program for economic recovery. True, it'll take time for the favorable effects of our program to be felt. So, we must begin now. The people are watching and waiting. They don't demand miracles. They do expect us to act. Let us act together.

—February 18, 1981 (from his speech to Congress detailing
his program for economic recovery)

Welfare's purpose should be to eliminate, as far as possible, the need for its own existence.

—January 7, 1970 (in an interview with the "Los Angeles Times")

No one who lived through the Great Depression can ever look upon an unemployed person with anything but compassion. To me, there is no greater tragedy than a breadwinner willing to work, with a job skill but unable to find a market for that job skill.

Back in those dark depression days I saw my father on a Christmas eve open what he thought was a Christmas greeting from his boss. Instead, it was the blue slip telling him he no longer had a job. The memory of him sitting there holding that slip of paper and then saying in a half whisper, 'That's quite a Christmas present,' it will stay with me as long as I live.

—March 31, 1976 (from his "To Restore America" speech, which included one of many references to his experiences during the Depression)

I hope the people on Wall Street will pay attention to the people on Main Street. If they do, they will see there is a rising tide of confidence in the future of America.

—Summer 1981

I have a special reason for wanting to solve this [economic] problem in a lasting way. I was 21 and looking for work in 1932, one of the worst years of the Great Depression. And I can remember one bleak night in the thirties when my father learned on Christmas Eve that he'd lost his job. To be young in my generation was to feel that your future had been mortgaged out from under you, and that's a tragic mistake we must never allow our leaders to make again.

—October 13, 1982 (in an address to the nation on the economy)

8

On America

Ronald Reagan's ascendancy came to be known as the Reagan Revolution. It featured a return of American morale, a boosting of the nation's military power, a reduced role of government, the rollback of numerous liberal agendas, and the escalation of the Cold War.

The term *Reagan Revolution* came from the fact that the Senate and the Congress also saw shocking reversals in the balance of power between the Republicans and Democrats. Many of the newly elected Republican congressmen had ridden to office on Reagan's coattails. They emulated his message and were swept in on a wave of good will and popular enthusiasm.

In his first inaugural address on January 20, 1981, which Reagan himself wrote, he addressed the country's economic malaise, arguing: "Government is not the solution to our

President Reagan giving the Inaugural Address from the U.S. Capitol, January 20, 1981

problems; government *is* the problem." The biggest news on the day of Reagan's inauguration was that the fifty-two U.S. hostages, held by Iran for 444 days, were set free.

An assassination attempt was made on Reagan's life on March 30, 1981. In the attempt, John Hinckley, Jr., shot the president, press secretary James Brady, and two other administration officials. The bullet pierced the president's left lung, and he was rushed to George Washington University Hospital. He had emergency surgery. In the operating room, Reagan joked with the surgeons, "I hope you're all Republicans!"

Though they were not, Joseph Giordano replied, "Today, Mr. President, we're all Republicans."

Reagan was successful in driving down inflation. It was 12.5 percent when he went into office, and it had been reduced to 4.4 percent when he left office. During his two terms, unemployment went from 7.1 percent down to 5.5 percent. Reagan implemented conservative policies based on supply-side economics. His administration fought for and won large, across-the-board tax cuts, which it argued would stimulate the

All great change in America begins at the dinner table.

—farewell address, January 11, 1989

Chaos outside the Washington Hilton Hotel after the assassination attempt on President Reagan. James Brady and police officer Thomas Delahanty lie wounded on the ground, March 30, 1981

economy. The federal income tax rates were lowered significantly with the signing of the bipartisan Economic Recovery Tax Act of 1981.

After the recession abated in 1982, the nation's gross domestic product (GDP) growth recovered and grew during his eight years in office at an annual rate of 3.4 percent per year.

President Reagan authorized the deployment of American peacekeeping forces to Beirut, Lebanon, where they were part of a multinational force during the Lebanese civil war. On October 23, 1983, a suicide bombing of a barracks in Beirut resulted in the deaths of 241 American servicemen. Reagan called the attack "despicable."

On October 25, 1983, President Reagan ordered U.S. forces to invade Grenada, where a 1979 coup had established a Marxist-Leninist government aligned with the Soviet Union and Cuba. A formal appeal from the Organisation of Eastern Caribbean States (OECS) led to the intervention by U.S. forces. In mid-December, after a new government was appointed by the governor-general, U.S. forces withdrew.

As a show of force and readiness, Reagan escalated the Cold War. He reversed Nixon's and Carter's policies of détente, and he ordered a massive buildup of the United

The Reagans honor the victims of the bombing of the U.S. Embassy in Beirut, Lebanon, at Andrews Air Force Base, Maryland, April 23, 1983

States military. His administration revived the B-1 bomber program and approved production of the MX "Peace-keeper" missile and the deployment of the Pershing II missile in West Germany, in response to Soviet nuclear threats.

President Reagan was the first American president ever to address the British Parliament. In his speech on June 8, 1982, in the Royal Gallery of the Palace of Westminster, he predicted that "the forward march of freedom and democracy will leave Marxism-Leninism on the ash-heap of history." On March 3, 1983, he again predicted that communism would collapse, stating: "Communism is another sad, bizarre chapter in human history whose last pages even now are being written."

The Reagan administration was very intent on defeating communism. It aided almost any anticommunist group in any communist or Soviet-backed government throughout Asia, Africa, and the Middle East. Its most famous success was the war in Afghanistan, in which the administration aided the rebels in defeating the mighty Soviet army. And Reagan's Star Wars missile defense system, also known as the Strategic Defense Initiative (SDI), was also believed to help hasten the end of the Cold War, as the Soviets became increasingly concerned that they could not keep pace.

I, in my own mind, have always thought of America as a place in the divine scheme of things that was set aside as a promised land. It was set here, and the price of admission was very simple: the means of selection was very simple as to how this land should be populated. Any place in the world and any person from those places; any person with the courage, with the desire to tear up their roots, to strive for freedom, to attempt and dare to live in a strange and foreign place, to travel halfway across the world was welcome here.

—from a commencement address at
Williams Woods College, June 1952

Excellence demands competition among students and among schools. And why not? We must always meet our obligation to those who would fall behind without our assistance. But let's remember, without a race, there can be no champion, no records broken, no excellence—in education or in any other walk of life.

—remarks to the National Catholic Education Association, April 15, 1982

The American dream is not that every man must be level with every other man. The American dream is that every man must be free to become whatever God intends he should become.

—from a speech to The Creative Society, 1968

There are no great limits to growth because there are no limits of human intelligence, imagination, and wonder.

President Reagan and Walter Mondale during the presidential debate on foreign policy, Louisville, Kentucky, October 7, 1984

9

On War and Peace

REAGAN'S OPPONENT IN THE 1984 PRESIDENTIAL election was Walter Mondale, the former vice president under Jimmy Carter. Questions arose whether Reagan was fit to be president for another term, citing his advanced age. Reagan confronted questions about his age during the second debate with Mondale, when Reagan quipped: "I will not make age an issue of this campaign. I am not going to exploit, for political purposes, my opponent's youth and inexperience," which generated laughter and applause from the audience.

That November, Reagan was re-elected in a landslide, winning forty-nine of fifty states. Reagan won a record 525 electoral votes, the most of any candidate in United States history, and garnered 58.8 percent of the popular vote to Mondale's 40.6 percent. He was sworn in as president for the second time on January 20, 1985.

On January 28, 1986, the space shuttle *Challenger* exploded just after takeoff, killing all seven astronauts aboard. On the night of the disaster, Reagan delivered a stirring speech in which he said: "The future doesn't belong to the faint-hearted; it belongs to the brave . . . We will never forget them, nor the last time we saw them, this morning, as they prepared for their journey and waved goodbye and slipped the surly bonds of Earth to touch the face of God."

By the mid-1980s, with the ascension of Mikhail Gorbachev, Ronald Reagan recognized the change in the direction of the Soviet leadership. Reagan now used détente and his larger-than-life leadership skills to forge a new kind of relationship with the Soviets. The Soviet Union at the time was struggling with the results of collectivized farming and the heavy debt burdens brought about by the arms race. Gorbachev and Reagan held four summit conferences between 1985 and 1988. Reagan believed that if he could persuade the Soviets to allow for

> We cannot play innocents abroad in a world that is not innocent.
>
> —State of the Union address, February 2, 1985

President Reagan addresses the nation from the Oval Office on national security (SDI speech), March 23, 1983

I call upon the scientific community in our country, those who gave us nuclear weapons, to turn their great talents now to the cause of mankind and world peace, to give us the means of rendering those nuclear weapons impotent and obsolete.

—address to the nation concerning the proposed Strategic Defense Initiative, March 23, 1983

more democracy and free speech, this would lead to reform and the end of communism.

On June 12, 1987, Reagan visited Berlin, and he went to the Berlin Wall, where he made a speech, challenging Gorbachev to go further, saying, "General Secretary Gorbachev, if you seek peace, if you seek prosperity for the Soviet Union and eastern Europe, if you seek liberalization, come here to this gate! Mr. Gorbachev, open this gate! Mr. Gorbachev, tear down this wall!"

When Reagan visited Moscow for the fourth summit in 1988, he was viewed as a celebrity by Russians. A journalist asked the president if he still considered the Soviet Union the evil empire. "No," he replied, "I was talking about another time, another era." At Gorbachev's request, Reagan gave a speech on free markets at the Moscow State University.

On November 9, 1989, The Berlin Wall was for all intents and purposes considered nonexistent, as people started to freely pass through the check points. Two years later, the Soviet Union collapsed.

"However willing Reagan might have been to fight communism by covert means," wrote Daniel McCarthy in the *New York Times*, "the elimination of nuclear weapons was his overriding objective—his 'dream.'"

No mother would ever willingly sacrifice her sons for territorial gain, for economic advantage, for ideology.

—speech at Moscow State University, May 31, 1988

Peace is not absence of conflict, it is the ability to handle conflict by peaceful means.

—toast at a United Nations luncheon, June 17, 1982

Of the four wars in my lifetime, none came about because the U. S. was too strong.

—remarks from the Republican National Convention, August 23, 1984

The person who agrees with you 80 percent of the time is a friend and an ally — not a 20 percent traitor.

—remark made in 1972

History teaches that wars begin when governments believe the price of aggression is cheap.

—address to the nation from the White House, January 16, 1984

Freedom is the right to question and change the established way of doing things. Cannot swords be turned to plowshares? Can we and all nations not live in peace? In our obsession with antagonisms of the moment, we often forget how much unites all the members of humanity. Perhaps we need some outside, universal threat to make us recognize this common bond. I occasionally think how quickly our differences worldwide would vanish if we were facing an alien threat from outside this world. And yet, I ask you, is not an alien force already among us? What could be more alien to the universal aspirations of our peoples than war and the threat of war?

—address to United Nations General Assembly, September 21, 1987

And make no mistake about it, this attack was not just against ourselves or the Republic of Korea. This was the Soviet Union against the world and the moral precepts which guide human relations among people everywhere. It was an act of barbarism born of a society which wantonly disregards individual rights and the value of human life and seeks constantly to expand and dominate other nations.

—from a televised speech following the Soviet downing of a South Korean airliner, September 5, 1983

A people free to choose will always choose peace.

—toast at a United Nations luncheon, June 17, 1982

President Reagan giving speech on the 40th anniversary of D-Day at Pointe du Hoc, Normandy, France, June 6, 1984

I believe with all my heart that our first priority must be world peace, and that use of force is always and only a last resort, when everything else has failed, and then only with regard to our national security.

—at the D-Day Commemoration in Normandy, France, June 6, 1984

I am an environmentalist.... I am for clean air.... I know Teddy Kennedy had fun at the Democratic convention when he said that I said that trees and vegetation caused 80 percent of the air pollution in this country. Well, now he was a little wrong about what I said. I didn't say 80 percent. I said 92 percent—93 percent, pardon me. And I didn't say air pollution, I said oxides of nitrogen. Growing and decaying vegetation in this land are responsible for 93 percent of the oxides of nitrogen.

—as quoted in the *New York Times*, October 9, 1980

We will always remember. We will always be proud. We will always be prepared, so we may always be free.

—remarks at Omaha Beach, June 6, 1984

Every country and every people has a stake in the Afghan resistance, for the freedom fighters of Afghanistan are defending principles of independence and freedom that form the basis of global security and stability.

—referring to groups who were resisting Soviet rule of Afghanistan, with U.S. support, in Proclamation 4908—Afghanistan Day, March 10, 1982

From Stettin on the Baltic to Varna on the Black Sea, the regimes planted by totalitarianism have had more than thirty years to establish their legitimacy. But none—not one regime—has yet been able to risk free elections. Regimes planted by bayonets do not take root . . . If history teaches anything, it teaches self-delusion in the face of unpleasant facts is folly . . . Our military strength is a prerequisite to peace, but let it be clear we maintain this strength in the hope it will never be used, for the ultimate determinant in the struggle that's now going on in the world will not be bombs and rockets but a test of wills and ideas, a trial of spiritual resolve, the values we hold, the beliefs we cherish, the ideals to which we are dedicated.

—speech to the House of Commons, June 8, 1982

President Reagan addressing British Parliament, London, England, July 8, 1982

The defense policy of the United States is based on a simple premise: The United States does not start fights. We will never be an aggressor. What if free people could live secure in the knowledge that their security did not rest upon the threat of instant U.S. retaliation to deter a Soviet attack, that we could intercept and destroy strategic ballistic missiles before they reached our own soil or that of our allies? I know this is a formidable, technical task, one that may not be accomplished before the end of this century. Yet, current technology has attained a level of sophistication where it's reasonable for us to begin this effort. It will take years, probably decades, of effort on many fronts. There will be failures and setbacks, just as there will be successes and breakthroughs. And as we proceed, we must remain constant in preserving the nuclear deterrent and maintaining a solid capability for flexible response. But isn't it worth every investment necessary to free the world from the threat of nuclear war? We know it is.

—address to the nation on defense and national security
(the "Star Wars Speech"), March 23, 1983

One hundred nations in the UN have not agreed with us on just about everything that's come before them, where we're involved, and it didn't upset my breakfast at all.

—reacting to international criticism of the U.S. invasion of Grenada, November 3, 1983

We will always remember. We will always be proud.
We will always be prepared, so we may always be
free. The only way there could be war is if they start
it; we're not going to start a war.

—declaring what he would tell Yuri Andropov, were he in the room,
December 6, 1983

Today we have done what we had to do. If necessary,
we shall do it again. It gives me no pleasure to say
that, and I wish it were otherwise . . . When our
citizens are abused or attacked anywhere in the
world on the direct orders of a hostile regime, we will
respond so long as I'm in this Oval Office . . . Despite
our repeated warnings, Qaddafi continued his
reckless policy of intimidation, his relentless pursuit
of terror. He counted on America to be passive. He
counted wrong.

—address to the nation on the United States air strike against Libya,
April 14, 1986

FAMILY LIFE

TOP LEFT: Ronald Reagan and Nancy Reagan on the set of film *Tropic Zone* in Hollywood, California. April 4, 1952.

TOP: RIGHT Newlyweds Ronald Reagan and Nancy Reagan cutting their wedding cake at the Holdens' house in Toluca Lake, California, March 4, 1952.

BOTTOM: Ronald Reagan and Nancy Reagan together at an unknown event, 1950s.

TOP: Ronald Reagan with Nancy Reagan at their home in Pacific Palisades, California, 1958.

MIDDLE: Ronald Reagan, son Ron, Nancy Reagan and daughter Patti outside their Pacific Palisades home in California. 1960.

BOTTOM: The Reagan Family at Rancho Del Cielo: (left to right) Michael Reagan, President Reagan, Cameron Reagan, Colleen Reagan, Mrs. Reagan, Ashley Marie Reagan, Ron Reagan, Doria Reagan, Paul Grilley, Patti Davis, August 17, 1985

On
Leadership

AFTER LEAVING OFFICE IN 1989, RONALD AND Nancy Reagan purchased a home in the Bel Air neighborhood of Los Angeles, this in addition to the Reagan ranch in Santa Barbara. They regularly attended Bel Air Presbyterian Church and occasionally made appearances on behalf of the Republican party.

The Ronald Reagan Presidential Library was dedicated and opened to the public on November 4, 1991. Five U.S. presidents were in attendance at the dedication ceremonies, as well as six first ladies. It was the first time ever that five U.S. presidents were gathered in the same location.

At the 1992 Republican national convention, Ronald Reagan made a well-received speech. He was warmly and

President Reagan and Mrs. Reagan breaking ground for the Library, November 21, 1988.

roundly cheered and was never more popular. During a tribute to him in Washington, D.C., on February 3, 1994, he gave his final speech in public, and on April 27, 1994, he made his last major public appearance, at the funeral of President Richard Nixon.

In August 1994, at the age of 83, Ronald Reagan was diagnosed with Alzheimer's disease. In November, he informed the nation via a handwritten letter, declaring, in part:

I have recently been told that I am one of the millions of Americans who will be afflicted with Alzheimer's Disease. . . . At the moment, I feel just fine. I intend to live the remainder of the years God gives me on this earth doing the things I have always done. . . . I now begin the journey that will lead me into the sunset of my life. I know that for America there will always be a bright dawn ahead. Thank you, my friends. May God always bless you.

Reagan's public appearances became much less frequent with the progression of the disease, and his family decided that he would live in quiet isolation.

"I think it is appropriate to talk about Ronald Reagan and his leadership for a number of reasons," said Edwin Meese III in 1999 at a speech at Ashland University, in

Ashland, Ohio. "Our position of world leadership was threatened, and many of the pundits at the time said that democracy had peaked and was on the downhill slide, and that capitalism was no longer dominant as a world force. . . . [Reagan] had campaigned on two major goals. The first was to revitalize the economy, and the second, to rebuild our military capability and restore our position in world leadership. And that is what he set out to do." Meese pointed out that Reagan, by the sheer force of his personality and conviction, helped to stem the tide against both the domestic economic woes of the United States and the spread of communism, eventually defeating both. "I believe that, as we move forward toward the next century, a

President Reagan riding his horse "Giminish" at Camp David, Maryland, May 14, 1983

careful look at the Reagan legacy and President Reagan's leadership can provide the guidelines for a future in which we have peace, freedom, and the flourishing of the human spirit, which will be a benefit not only to the United States but the whole world."

If all of this seems like a great deal of trouble, think what's at stake. We are faced with the most evil enemy mankind has known in his long climb from the swamp to the stars.

—from a speech in support of presidential candidate Barry Goldwater, October 27, 1964

There can be no security anywhere in the free world if there is no fiscal and economic stability within the United States. Those who ask us to trade our freedom for the soup kitchen of the welfare state are architects of a policy of accommodation.

—in an interview with *Fortune* magazine, September 15, 1986

Surround yourself with the best people you can find, delegate authority, and don't interfere.

—remark in *Fortune* magazine, September 15, 1986

I have never given a litmus test to anyone that I have appointed to the bench. . . . I feel very strongly about those social issues, but I also place my confidence in the fact that the one thing that I do seek are judges that will interpret the law and not write the law. We've had too many examples in recent years of courts and judges legislating. They're not interpreting what the law says and whether someone has violated it or not. In too many instances, they have been actually legislating by legal decree what they think the law should be, and that I don't go for. And I think that the two men that we're just talking about here, Rehnquist and Scalia, are interpreters of the Constitution and the law.

—interview with the *Los Angeles Times*, June 23, 1986

The Reagan family at their house in Pacific Palisades, California. From left to right: Patti Davis, Nancy Reagan, Ronald Reagan, Michael Reagan, Maureen Reagan, Ron Reagan and dog "Pogo," 1976.

A troubled and afflicted mankind looks to us, pleading for us to keep our rendezvous with destiny; that we will uphold the principles of self-reliance, self-discipline, morality, and above all, responsible liberty for every individual that we will become that shining city on a hill. They tell us we must learn to live with less, and teach our children that their lives will be less full and prosperous than ours have been; that the America of the coming years will be a place where—because of our past excesses—it will be impossible to dream and make those dreams come true. I don't believe that. And, I don't believe you do, either. That is why I am seeking the presidency. I cannot and will not stand by and see this great country destroy itself. Our leaders attempt to blame their failures on circumstances beyond their control, on false estimates by unknown, unidentifiable experts who rewrite modern history in an attempt to convince us our high standard of living—the result of thrift and hard work—is somehow selfish extravagance which we must renounce as we join in sharing scarcity. I don't agree that our nation must resign itself to inevitable decline, yielding its proud position to other hands. I am totally unwilling to see this country fail in its obligation to itself and to the other free peoples of the world.

—from the announcement of candidacy for U.S. president,
   November 13, 1979

President Reagan with Chairman of Liberia Samuel Doe on the White House colonnade, August 17, 1982

11

Humor and Wit

RONALD REAGAN WAS CALLED "The Great Communicator," and there is a reason so many politicians have marveled at his gift for connecting with the American people. Reagan's gifts for speaking were incredible. He was always good at giving a speech. With a little twinkle in his eye, he might tell a joke or story, but he could hit home his points when he wanted to. He was very good at reading from a teleprompter but was equally good at making it look effortless.

He had a quick wit. Whether it was a rebuttal in a major debate or a funny one-liner at a news conference, Reagan was comfortable in his own skin, comfortable with himself. And the American people sensed that.

Nothing seemed to stick to the "Teflon President," which was another one of his nicknames. "As a young congresswoman, I got the idea of calling President Reagan the 'Teflon President' while fixing eggs for my kids. He had a Teflon coat like the pan," Patricia Schroeder told *USA Today*

President Reagan at a rally for Texas Republican candidates in Irving, Texas, October 11, 1982

years later. "Why was Reagan so blame-free? The answer can be found in the label that did stick to him—'The Great Communicator.' Reagan's ability to connect with Americans was coveted by every politician. He could deliver a speech with such sincerity. And his staff was brilliant in playing up his strengths. They made sure the setting for any speech perfectly captured, re-emphasized, and embraced the theme of that speech. . . . He came across with that Irish twinkle."

Reagan had developed a bond with the American people. He was called The Great Communicator because he was able to sell his programs by using simple words and ideas to sell much more complex ideas or programs. But he was always effective.

> You know, in a few months I'm going to be out of work, and I thought I might as well audition.
>
> —from a broadcast, September 30, 1988

One of Reagan's main weapons in all of this was his ability to tell a joke or story, or to come back with a funny quip or quote. While he took his job seriously, he could also, at times, while still being presidential, poke fun at himself and get people to laugh with him. This was one of his greatest strengths.

"Despite his stern rhetoric, Reagan is almost never visibly angered, even by the most hostile questions, and banters easily with practically anyone; he and his wife, Nancy, have made a ritual of passing out candy to reporters on campaign planes and buses. The old entertainer usually seeks to entertain his companions, too," reported *Time* magazine. "On a campaign bus driving through a heavy snow in New Hampshire, he started out with a labored joke: 'If anyone hears dogs barking, it's because the next leg will be done by sled.'"

When an assassination attempt was made on his life, reports of his quip, when they brought him into the operating room, "I hope you're all Republicans," immediately swept over the airwaves. People chuckled and marveled at a man who, so near death, still maintained his sense of humor. If he could be that level-headed under such personal duress, how could he not do well under the others pressures of the office?

"To sit back hoping that someday, some way, someone will make things right is to go on feeding the crocodile, hoping he will eat you last—but eat you he will."

I've never been able to understand why a Republican contributor is a 'fat cat' and a Democratic contributor of the same amount of money is a 'public-spirited philanthropist.'

I've often said there's nothing better for the inside of a man than the outside of a horse.

—remark made in Nebraska, 1987

If the federal government had been around when the Creator was putting His hand to this state, Indiana wouldn't be here. It'd still be waiting for an environmental impact statement.

—address made to the Indiana state legislature, February 9, 1982

❧

You can tell a lot about a fellow's character by his way of eating jelly beans.

—as quoted in the *Observer*, March 29, 1981

❧

Before I refuse to take your questions, I have an opening statement.

But there are advantages to being elected president. The day after I was elected, I had my high school grades classified Top Secret.

—remarks at high school commencement exercises,
Glassboro, New Jersey, June 19, 1986

If we love our country, we should also love our countrymen.

Life is one grand, sweet song,
so start the music.

༺⁓༻

My philosophy of life is that if we make up our mind

what we are going to make of our lives, then work hard

toward that goal, we never lose—somehow we win out.

Honey, I forgot to duck.

—spoken to Nancy Reagan following his assassination
attempt, March 30, 1981

I have left orders to be awakened at any time in case of national emergency, even if I'm in a cabinet meeting.

—said often during his presidency

When you see all that rhetorical smoke billowing up from the Democrats . . . well, ladies and gentleman, I'd follow the example of their nominee: don't inhale.

—at the Republican National Convention, August 17, 1992

*It's true, hard work never killed anyone,
but I figure, why take the chance?*

—on his relaxed approach to work

I'm not smart enough to lie.

—response when asked what qualified him to be president

*My fellow Americans, I'm pleased to tell you today
that I've signed legislation that will outlaw Russia
forever. We begin bombing in five minutes.*

—joking, unwittingly into an open mic, just before a speech, August 1984

Thomas Jefferson made a comment about the presidency
and age. He said that one should not worry about one's exact
chronological age in reference to his ability to perform one's
task. And ever since he told me that, I stopped worrying.

—remarks at the Annual Salute to Congress Dinner, February 4, 1981

Intelligence reports say he — Castro — is very worried about me. I'm very worried that we can't come up with something to justify his worrying.

—from the White House diary, February 11, 1981

Fidel Castro, president of Cuba, at a meeting of the United Nations General Assembly, September 22, 1960

I am not worried about the deficit. It is big enough to take care of itself.

—joke made at the Gridiron Club annual dinner, March 24, 1984

I want you to know that also I will not make age an issue of this campaign. I am not going to exploit, for political purposes, my opponent's youth and inexperience.

—debate with Walter Mondale, October 21, 1984

I don't know. I've never played a governor.

—response when asked what kind of governor he would be, 1966

I'm afraid I can't use a mule. I have several hundred up on Capitol Hill.

—refusing a gift of a mule

What does an actor know about politics?

—criticizing Ed Asner for opposing American foreign policy

What makes him think a middle-aged actor, who's played with a chimp, could have a future in politics?

—on Clint Eastwood's bid to become mayor of Carmel, California

Diplomacy, of course, is a subtle and nuanced craft,
so much so that it's said that when the most wily
diplomat of the nineteenth century passed away,
other diplomats asked, on reports of his death,
"What do you suppose the old fox meant by that?"

—address to United Nations General Assembly, September 21, 1987

⌇

Facts are stupid things—
stubborn things, I should say.

—address to the Republican National Convention, August 15, 1988

A hippie is someone who walks like Tarzan, looks like Jane, and smells like Cheetah.

Reagan's Legacy

Ronald Reagan died at his home in Bel Air, California, on June 5, 2004. "My family and I would like the world to know that President Ronald Reagan has passed away after ten years of Alzheimer's disease at ninety-three years of age. We appreciate everyone's prayers," said Nancy Reagan in a press release.

President George W. Bush declared June 11 a national day of mourning. From all over the world came tributes to the man who had defeated communism. Reagan's body was taken to a funeral home in Santa Monica, California. On June 7, his body was taken to the Ronald Reagan Presidential Library. His body lay in repose in the library lobby until June 9; over 100,000 people viewed the coffin.

Nancy Reagan, escorted by Major General Galen Jackman, arrives at the internment of her husband at the Ronald Reagan Presidential Library, Simi Valley, California, June 11, 2004

Ronald Reagan's casket is carried past President George W. Bush and four former U.S. presidents to the State Funeral at the National Cathedral, June 11, 2004

On June 9, Reagan's body was flown to Washington, D.C., where he became the tenth United States president to lie in state. In the thirty-four hours that he lay in state, 104,684 people filed past the coffin.

On June 11, a state funeral was conducted in the Washington National Cathedral and was presided over by President George W. Bush. Eulogies were given by former

British Prime Minister Margaret Thatcher, former Canadian Prime Minister Brian Mulroney, and Presidents George H. W. Bush and George W. Bush. Also in attendance were Mikhail Gorbachev, British Prime Minister Tony Blair, German Chancellor Gerhard Schröder, Italian Prime Minister Silvio Berlusconi, and interim presidents Hamid Karzai of Afghanistan, and Ghazi al-Yawer of Iraq, as well as many other world leaders.

Reagan was then flown back to the Ronald Reagan Presidential Library in California, where was interred in his final resting place. He is the second longest-lived president in U.S. history, having lived 93 years and 120 days, just 45 days fewer than Gerald Ford. He was the first United States president to die in the twenty-first century, and his was the first state funeral in the United States since that of President Lyndon B. Johnson in 1973.

"I know in my heart that man is good, that what is right will always eventually triumph, and that there is purpose and worth to each and every life," are the words inscribed at his burial site.

History will give Reagan great credit for standing for principles.

—George H. W. Bush

Pride in our country, respect for our armed services, a healthy appreciation for the dangers beyond our borders, an insistence that there was no easy equivalence between East and West—in all this, I had no quarrel with Reagan. And when the Berlin Wall came tumbling down, I had to give the old man his due, even if I never gave him my vote.

—President Barack Obama

An excellent leader of our nation during challenging times at home and abroad.

—Gerald Ford

This is a sad hour in the life of America. . . . Ronald Reagan won America's respect with his greatness, and won its love with his goodness. . . . He leaves behind a nation he restored and a world he helped save. . . . Because of his leadership, the world laid to rest an era of fear and tyranny.

—President George W. Bush

President Reagan was a formidable political campaigner, who provided . . . unshakable beliefs and was able to express them effectively, both in America and abroad.

—President James Carter

He believed that freedom was a universal value … that people everywhere wished to be free, and … the Cold War would end.

—President William Jefferson Clinton

An excellent leader of our nation during challenging times at home and abroad.

—President Gerald Ford

A determined opponent of communism . . . he played an important role in bringing an end to communism and to the artificial division of Europe imposed after the Second World War. . . . This process culminated in the accession of ten new member-states to the European Union at the beginning of May this year.

—Irish Prime Minister and European Union President Bertie Ahern

At home his vision and leadership restored national self-confidence and brought some significant changes to U.S. politics while abroad the negotiation of arms control agreements in his second term and his statesmanlike pursuit of more stable relations with the Soviet Union helped bring about the end of the Cold War.

—British Prime Minister Tony Blair

President Reagan, in his long and fruitful life, was witness to . . . facing important challenges, including the end of the Cold War.

—Mexican President Vincente Fox

∽

I take the death of Ronald Reagan very hard. He was a man whom fate set by me in perhaps the most difficult years at the end of the twentieth century. He has already entered history as a man who was instrumental in bringing about the end of the Cold War. . . . It was his goal and his dream to end his term and enter history as a peacemaker.

—Former Soviet Leader Mikhail Gorbachev

He salutes the memory of a great man of state who, through the force of his convictions and his commitment in favor of democracy, will leave a profound mark on history.

—French President Jacques Chirac

True, Reagan was a man of the right. But, while adhering to his convictions, with which one could agree or disagree, he was not dogmatic; he was looking for negotiations and cooperation.

—Soviet Prime Minister Mikhail Gorbachev

President Reagan was the Churchill of his era.
His commitment to the principles of freedom and
democracy and his boundless optimism for humanity
will remain an inspiration for us all.

—Canadian Prime Minister Stephen Harper

I recall with deep gratitude the late president's unwavering commitment to the service of the nation and to the cause of freedom as well as his abiding faith in the human and spiritual values which ensure a future of solidarity, justice, and peace in our world.

—Pope John Paul II

Ronald Reagan, in my view, was the greatest of post–World War II American presidents. More than anybody else, he followed the policies that led to the collapse of the Soviet Union, the end of the Cold War, and the final victory of a more free-market approach to the management of economies over the centrally planned approach of the old eastern states.... His greatest legacy will be the end of Soviet communism.

—Australian Prime Minister John Howard

This is an enormously sad day. President Reagan was one of the towering figures of our time, and the man who, with Margaret Thatcher, won the Cold War for the West. ... We, in Great Britain, as in so many other places around the world, owe him an everlasting debt.

—British Conservative Party Leader Michael Howard

During the arduous period of the Cold War,
President Reagan showed great leadership and
contributed tremendously to the advancement of
democracy and free-market economy. In addition,
President Reagan always placed a top priority on the
maintenance of a sound Japan–U.S. alliance.

—Japanese Prime Minister Junichiro Koizumi

President Reagan's leadership served to define an era of sweeping geo-political change … He helped lay the foundations for the end of the Cold War … His wit, warmth, and unique capacity to communicate helped to make him one of the most influential figures in the second half of the 20th century.

—former Canadian Prime Minister Paul Martin

Ronald Reagan had a higher claim than any other leader to have won the Cold War for liberty, and he did it without a shot being fired.

—British Prime Minster Margaret Thatcher

Ronald Reagan was a transformational president who made an enormous difference in our lives by leading the West to victory in the Cold War and allowing free people to watch the disintegration of the Soviet Union.

—Canadian Prime Minister Brian Mulroney

He was a great president who guided the Cold War toward a victory for freedom against communism. . . . He would use his skillful humor and leadership to steer them to success.

—Japanese Prime Minister Yasuhiro Nakasone

President and Mrs. Reagan walk together at the Pometta residence in Geneva , Switzerland, November 17, 1985

Hungary and Europe do not forget Ronald Reagan's help and his support for the former communist countries.

—Hungarian Prime Minister Viktor Orbán

His commitment to overcoming the East-West conflict and his vision of a free and united Europe helped pave the way for those developments that ultimately enabled Germany also to regain its unity.

—German Chancellor Gerhard Schröder

⌒⌒

When he saw injustice, he wanted to do away with it. He saw communism, and he wanted to put an end to it.

—Polish President Lech Walesa

Recommended Reading

Books by Ronald Reagan

Where's the Rest of Me? (1965)

An American Life: The Autobiography (1990)

Reagan, In His Own Hand: The Writings of Ronald Reagan That Reveal His Revolutionary Vision for America (2001)

Reagan: A Life in Letters (2003)

The Reagan Diaries, edited by Douglas Brinkley (2007)

Books by Nancy Reagan

My Turn: The Memoirs of Nancy Reagan (1989)

I Love You, Ronnie: The Letters of Ronald Reagan to Nancy Reagan (2000)

Books by Reagan Administration Officials

Anderson, Martin. *Revolution: The Reagan Legacy* (1990). By a top aide.

Deaver, Michael and Mickey Herskowitz. *Behind the Scenes.* (1987). By a top aide.

Deaver, Michael. *A Different Drummer: My Thirty Years with Ronald Reagan* (2001). By a top aid (with a foreword by Nancy Reagan).

Gergen, David. *Eyewitness to Power: The Essence of Leadership.* (2000). By a speechwriter.

Haig, Alexander. *Inner Circles: How America Changed the World* (1994). By Reagan's first secretary of state.

Regan, Donald. *For the Record: From Wall Street to Washington* (1988). By Reagan's secretary of the treasury (1981–85), and chief of staff (1985–87), who is seen as a fall guy for the administration in the Iran-Contra affair.

Shultz, George P. *Turmoil and Triumph: My Years As Secretary of State* (1993). By Reagan's second secretary of state.

Weinberger, Caspar. *In the Arena: A Memoir of the 20th Century* (1991). By Reagan's secretary of defense.